Success in M[asked] Test Booster

Rowena Onions
Chris Onions
Jacqueline Pendergast
Garry Pendergast
Series Editor: Jayne de Courcy

AGES 10–11

Contents

Collins Educational
An Imprint of HarperCollinsPublishers

The ⭐3 Steps to Success ...

Step 1 — Test practice papers

★ *Success in Maths: Test Booster* gives your child the opportunity to practise answering the type of Test papers that are set in the Maths National Test at the end of Key Stage 2. Both Test papers span a range of Maths topics. Children are allowed to use a calculator in Test B but not in Test A or the Mental Maths Test.

★ All the questions in this book are taken from past National Test papers. You can use the book to give 'test practice', to check on the level at which your child is currently performing, or to diagnose difficulties.

Step 2 — Detailed answers and guidance

★ In the *Answers and Guidance* sections, the authors, who are KS2 Test Examiners, provide step-by-step solutions to each question.

★ These can be used either to help your child work through a question which has caused difficulty, or to check that the method your child used was an efficient one.

Step 3 — Extra revision

★ In the *Answers and Guidance*, the 'Inside the Maths' box provides a description of the Maths knowledge and skills needed to answer each question. This will help you to identify any areas of Maths which are causing your child difficulty.

★ References are given to the chapters in *Success in Maths Books 1–4* where the relevant skills and knowledge are revised.

★ In this way, you can diagnose where your child is having difficulty and find appropriate help quickly and easily. <u>No other Test Practice book provides this amount of cross-referencing and support</u>. It will help your child improve their performance in the KS2 Maths National Test.

Helping your child

★ In Tests A and B, encourage your child to write down their working. This will help them to be more accurate and will allow you to identify any difficulties. In the actual Test, showing working may give your child a mark even if a mistake is made in the calculation.

★ Don't set your child papers A and B on the same day. In the Maths National Test they will be on different days.

★ The Test allows 45 minutes for each paper. Your child needs to work at the right speed to complete each paper. At home, tell your child that they have 45 minutes to complete the paper, then time how long it takes them. If your child is working accurately but slowly, they need practice in answering questions faster. *Success in Maths Books 1–4* have lots of timed practice questions that will help your child to work faster.

★ When you read the questions in the Mental Test to your child, you need to be careful that you allow only the stated amount of time for writing the answer to each question.

★ Your child needs to complete the Mental Maths answer sheet included in this book while you are reading out the questions.

Marks and levels

★ Once your child has completed both papers and the Mental Test, add up their marks to work out the level they would probably achieve.

★ 20–39 marks would gain a level 3, 40–59 marks would gain a level 4 and 60 marks and above would gain a level 5.

Note to teachers

★ This book, and the other five titles in the *Success in Maths* series, are designed for use at home and in school in years 5 and 6.

★ The *Test Booster* will provide invaluable test practice for children in Year 6 who are approaching their Maths National Test at the end of Key Stage 2. It will also provide diagnostic support to teachers of children in Years 5 and 6 by identifying areas of mathematical weakness. Using the cross-referenced material from *Success in Maths Books 1–4* will help raise children's performance in their Maths National Test.

You MAY NOT use a calculator to answer any questions in this test.

1 This is a number triangle with some numbers missing.
The numbers along each edge must add up to **90**.

Put **all** the numbers **20**, **30**, **50** and **60** in the circles to make the totals correct.

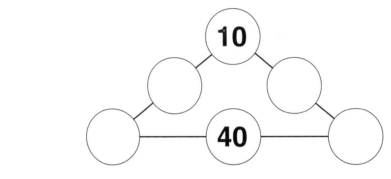

1 mark

2 Draw **one line** from each shape to the rectangle which has the **same area**.

One is done for you.

 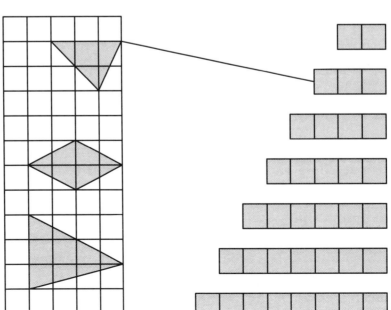

1 mark

1 mark

3 This table shows the cost of sending a letter.

Mass	Cost in pence	
	first class	second class
up to 60 g	26	20
61 g to 100 g	39	31
101 g to 150 g	49	38
151 g to 200 g	60	45
201 g to 250 g	70	55

Paul is sending a letter.

It costs **38p second class**.

How much would it cost him to send it **first class**?

p

1 mark

Jenny has a letter with a mass of **170 g**.

What does it cost to send it **first class**?

p

1 mark

4 Write what the **two missing digits** could be.

6 2 + 9 5 = 757

1 mark

5

5 Three children start with **50p** each.

Charlie   Susan   Peter

Charlie gives Susan **15p**.

How much do **Charlie** and **Susan** each have now?

	p

Charlie

	p

Susan

1 mark

Peter gives **half** of his 50p to Susan.

How much does **Peter** have left?

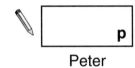

	p

Peter

1 mark

6 Use a ruler to draw the **reflection** of this shape in the mirror line.
You may use a mirror or tracing paper.

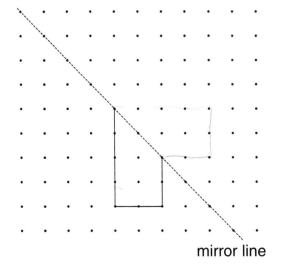

mirror line

1 mark

6

7 In the circle write **+**, **−**, **×** or **÷**
to make the calculation correct.

✎ **18** ◯ **3** **×** **5** **=** **30**

8 Here are six triangles. One of them is an **equilateral** triangle.

Put a tick (✓) in the **equilateral triangle**.

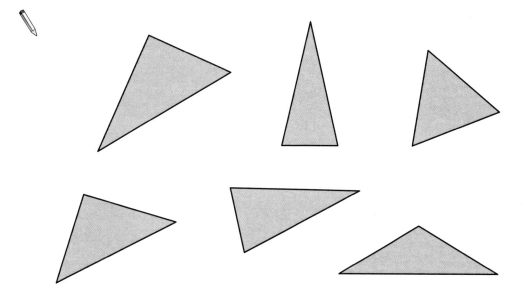

1 mark

Write **one property** which makes **equilateral** triangles **different**
from **all** other triangles.

✎ ....

....

....

9 Here are some shapes on a grid.

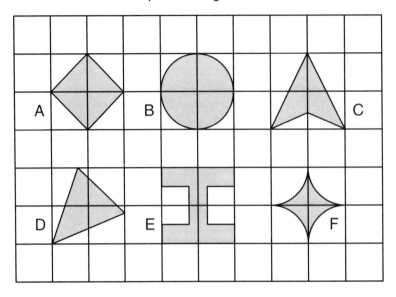

Which shape has the **longest perimeter**?

1 mark

Which shape has the **largest area**?

1 mark

10 Here is a number sequence.
Write the **missing** number.

 1   3   6   10

1 mark

Explain how you worked it out.

....

....

....

....

1 mark

11 Rob has some number cards.

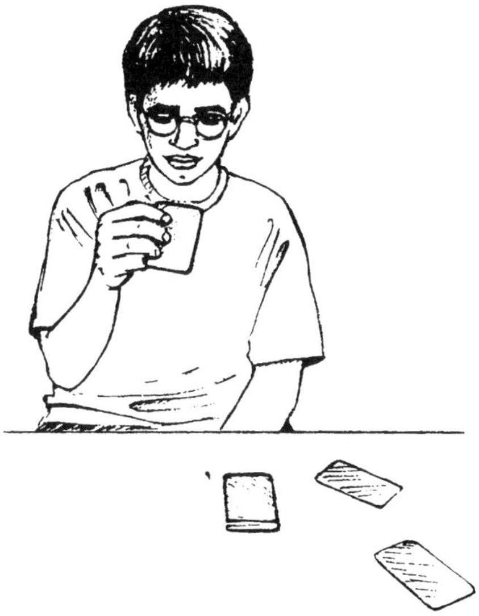

He holds up a card.

He says,

'If I multiply the number on this card by 5, the answer is 35.'

What is the number on the card?

☐

1 mark

He holds up a different card.

He says,

'If I divide the number on this card by 6, the answer is 4.'

What is the number on the card?

☐

1 mark

12 Write in the missing digit.

The answer **does not** have a **remainder**.

$$\begin{array}{r} 26 \\ 3\overline{)\square 8} \end{array}$$

☐

1 mark

13

Five children collect money to plant trees.

Here is a bar chart of the amounts they have raised so far.

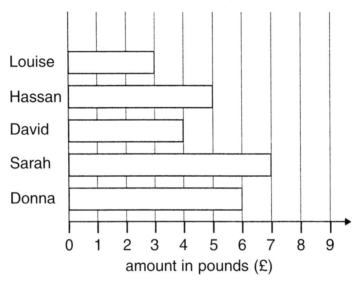

amount in pounds (£)

Their target is **£40 altogether**.

How much **more** money do they need to reach the target?

Show your **working**. You may get a mark.

£

2 marks

14 This ring is made of **regular pentagons**, with sides of **5 centimetres**.

5 cm

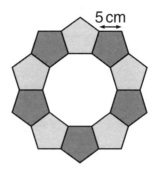

What is the **length** of the **outer edge** of the ring?

cm

1 mark

Here is part of a new ring.

It is made of **squares** and **triangles**.

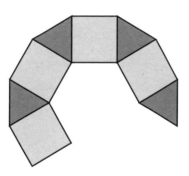

The pattern is continued to complete the ring.

What is the **total** number of **squares** used in the complete ring?

1 mark

15 Megan makes a sequence of numbers starting with **100**.

She **subtracts 45** each time.

Write the next **two** numbers in the sequence.

1 mark

100   55   10

1 mark

16 This diagram shows the proportions of waste by weight a family throws away in one year.

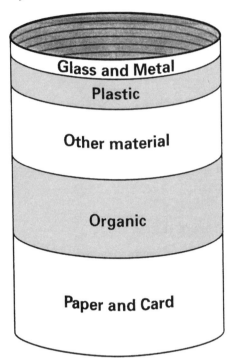

Estimate what **fraction** of the waste is **organic**.

1 mark

The family throws away about **35 kilograms of plastic** a year.

Use the diagram to estimate the weight of **glass and metal** they throw away.

kg

1 mark

The family throws away **130 kg** of paper and card.

70% of this is **newspapers**.

What is the weight of **newspapers**?

Show your **working**. You may get a mark.

kg

2 marks

17 Lee has two spinners.

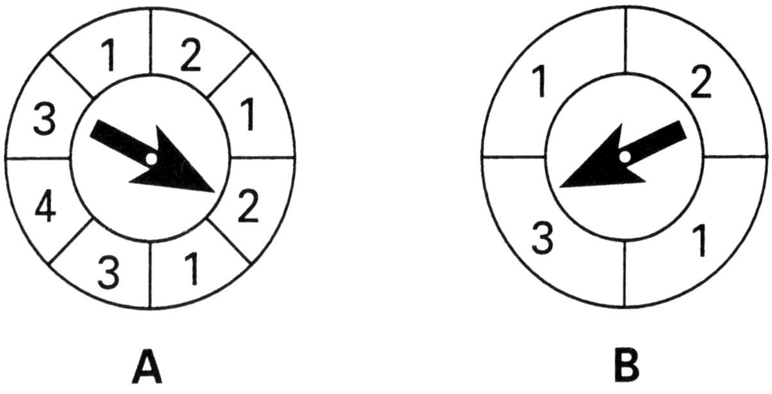

A   B

What is the probability of spinning a **4** on **spinner A**?

Write your answer as a fraction.

1 mark

On which spinner is he **more likely** to get a **1**?

Give a reason for your answer.

....

....

....

1 mark

Lee says,

'I am equally likely to get a 2 on a spinner A as on spinner B.'

Explain why he is correct.

....

....

....

1 mark

18 Circle the **two** numbers which add up to **1**.

0.1   0.65   0.99   0.45   0.35

1 mark

19 Eggs are put in **trays of 12**.

The trays are packed in boxes.

Each **box** contains **180 eggs**.

How many **trays** are in each **box**?

Show your **working**. You may get a mark.

2 marks

20 Calculate **268 × 53**

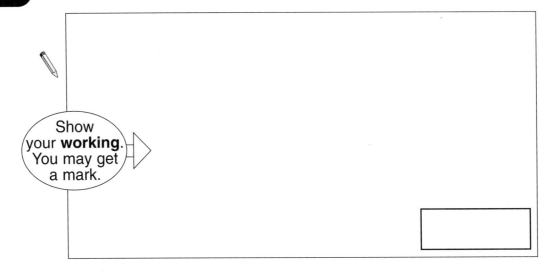

Show your **working**. You may get a mark.

2 marks

Test A

Question 1

Answer

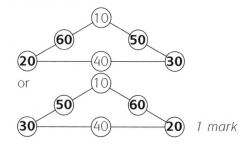

1 mark

Inside the Maths

You needed to be able to:

 use + and – in number problems

work carefully and systematically.

See Collins Success in Maths Book 4, Chapters 4 and 12 Solving problems.

How to work out the answer

 Look at the bottom row first.

You know that you cannot put either 60 or 50 in this row because:

$60 + 40 = 100$ (too many)

and $50 + 40 = 90$ (already at the target before adding the last number)

so the bottom row is **20** 40 **30** or **30** 40 **20**

 Now look at the remaining missing numbers, remembering that the numbers along each edge must add up to 90.

10 + 20 = 30 so you need 60 to make 90.	10 **60** **50** 20 40 30	10 + 30 = 40 so you need 50 to make 90.

or

10 + 30 = 40 so you need 50 to make 90.	10 **50** **60** 30 40 20	10 + 20 = 30 so you need 60 to make 90.

Question 2

Answer

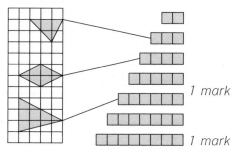

1 mark

1 mark

Inside the Maths

You needed:

 to understand how to calculate areas by counting squares.

See Collins Success in Maths Book 2, Chapter 5 Area.

How to work out the answer

 This is the same for both shapes.

Count the squares in the shape. Start with any whole squares.

 Either count any part squares which are larger than half and ignore any that are less than half…

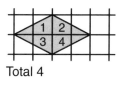

Total 4

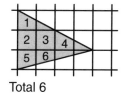

Total 6

or put parts of squares together in your head to make whole squares. The illustrations are coloured to help you to see which part squares go together.

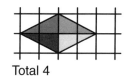

Total 4

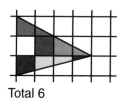

Total 6

Answers and Guidance

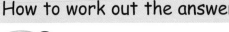

Answer

How to work out the answer

a) 49p   *1 mark*

 Look down the column headed 'second class' until you find a stamp that costs 38p – use your finger to keep your place.

STEP 2 Look across from this figure to the figure in the column headed 'first class'. You will see that it costs 49p.

Answer

How to work out the answer

b) 60p   *1 mark*

 Look at the column headed 'mass' and identify that 170 g lies within the 151 g to 200 g band or range. Keep this place marked.

 Look across from here to the figure in the column headed 'first class'. You will see that it costs 60p.

Inside the Maths

You needed to:

 be able to read a table

be very careful to look along

know about the relative size of numbers in order to see where they lie in a range

 be very careful to look along rows and down columns without losing your place or making errors in reading or writing the numbers.

See *Collins Success in Maths Book 1*, Chapter 2 Using timetables and *Book 4*, Chapter 10 Interpreting data.

Answer

How to work out the answer

Any one of the following.

162 + **5**95 = 757

262 + **4**95 = 757

362 + **3**95 = 757

462 + **2**95 = 757

562 + **1**95 = 757   *1 mark*

 Start at the right end of the number sentence and add what you have. It is easier if you write it down like this.

```
   62
+  95
   57
  1
```

You can see that there is a carrying figure.

 Choose any two numbers to put in the hundreds position but remember that when you add them **and** the carrying figure, your answer must be 7.

```
e.g.    262
      + 495
        757
       1        (add the carrying figure)
```

Inside the Maths

You needed to be able to:

 add two digit numbers in a number problem.

See *Collins Success in Maths Book 1*, Chapter 10 Solving problems.

Question 5

Answer

How to work out the answer

a) 35p   65p
   Charlie Susan   *1 mark*

 Identify the sums that you need to do as:

50p – 15p and 50p + 15p

 If you can do this in your head, that's great! If not, write down the sums. You may well find it easier to write them like this:

$$\begin{array}{r} 50 \\ -15 \\ \hline 35 \end{array} \qquad \begin{array}{r} 50 \\ +15 \\ \hline 65 \end{array}$$

Be careful not to make a mistake in the subtraction.

Answer

How to work out the answer

b) 25p   Peter   *1 mark*

 You probably know that half of 50 is 25 but if not, you must divide 50 by 2.

 $2\overline{)50}^{\,25}$

Inside the Maths

You needed to be able to:

 identify the mathematics that you need to solve the problem

 add, subtract and do simple division accurately

find half of a given number.

See Collins Success in Maths Book 1, Chapter 4 Missing numbers and Chapter 10 Solving problems.

Question 6

Answer

How to work out the answer

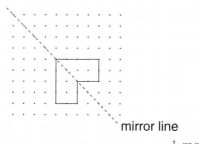

mirror line

1 mark

 Either: Use a mirror to see where the reflection lies.

Check the length of the sides of the reflected shape.

The long side should be 4 spaces.

The short side should be 2 spaces.

The width should be 2 spaces.

Or: Trace the shape.

Remember to turn your tracing paper over.

Mark the new points by pressing hard through the tracing paper.

Use a ruler to draw your new shape.

 mirror line

Inside the Maths

You needed to know about:

 reflective symmetry.

See Collins Success in Maths Book 1, Chapter 11 Reflective symmetry and Book 3, Chapter 10 Reflective symmetry.

Answers and Guidance

Question 7

Answer

18 ⊝ 3 × 5 = 30   *1 mark*

Inside the Maths

You needed to:

- know your tables thoroughly
- be able to use multiplication and division facts to solve problems.

See Collins *Success in Maths Book 1*, Chapter 5 Using multiplication and *Book 2*, Chapter 2 Division.

How to work out the answer

STEP 1 Using your knowledge of the 5 times table, you can see that 18 ◯ 3 must be 6. This is because 6 × 5 = 30.

STEP 2 Using your knowledge of the 6 times or 3 times table you can work out that 18 ÷ 3 = 6 so 18 ÷ 3 × 5 = 30.

Question 8

Answer

a)

                                 1 mark

b) You could have given any of the following answers.
An equilateral triangle has:
three sides of equal length
three equal angles
three angles of 60°
three lines of reflective symmetry.   *1 mark*

How to work out the answer

STEP 1 Use what you know about triangles to identify the one you need. Then describe the triangle.

If you have used slightly different language, it probably doesn't matter. Ask an adult if you are not sure that what you have said is clear and correct.

Answers such as 'three angles', 'three sides', 'three angles that add up to 180°' are **not** correct because they are true of all triangles. The question asks you to give a property that makes equilateral triangles different from all other triangles.

Inside the Maths

You needed:

- to know the properties of an equilateral triangle
- to be able to express your ideas clearly
- to be able to spell the mathematical vocabulary used.

See *Collins Success in Maths Book 1*, Chapter 3 Drawing 2D shapes and *Book 2*, Chapter 1 Properties of shape.

Question 9

Answer

a) E   *1 mark*

How to work out the answer

STEP 1 Recall that the perimeter is the distance around the outside of a shape.

STEP 2 In this question, shape E clearly has the longest perimeter – you can see this just by looking carefully.
If the differences are not as obvious in other questions, you would need to measure them.

Question 9 continued ...

Answer

b) B *1 mark*

Inside the Maths

You needed to:

 know the meaning of the mathematical words 'area' and 'perimeter'

 be able to make comparisons between different shapes.

See *Collins Success in Maths Book 3*, Chapter 8 Area and perimeter

How to work out the answer

STEP 1 Recall that the area is the amount of space within the shape.

STEP 2 This is, perhaps, not as easy to see in this question. Notice, however, that each shape is contained within 4 squares. Now look at the amount of these squares that is not shaded.

STEP 3 Shapes A, C, D and F have a lot of white space around them.

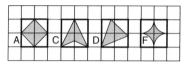

STEP 4 Compare shapes B and E.

By looking carefully you can see that E has more space around it than B so B has the largest area of all the shapes.

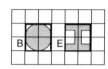

Question 10

Answer

a) 1 3 6 10 **15** *1 mark*

How to work out the answer

STEP 1 Work out the gaps between the numbers:

1   3   6   10
     + 2   + 3   + 4

STEP 2 Identify that the rule is 'add one more each time'.

STEP 3 Add 5 to the last number in the sequence.

1   3   6   10   15
     + 2   + 3   + 4   + 5

Answer

b) Your answer needs to give an explanation that is like this one.

'The gap between the numbers increases by one each time.'

1 mark

How to work out the answer

Ask an adult to check if your answer to part (b) is clear.

You might also have known that this sequence of numbers has a particular name: they are called triangular numbers. If you wrote 'because they are **triangular numbers**' this is also correct.

Inside the Maths

You needed to be able to:

 work out the rules for a number sequence and calculate the missing number

 write clear mathematical explanations

 spell the words used when talking about sequences, such as 'increase' and 'decrease'.

See *Collins Success in Maths Book 1*, Chapter 1 Number patterns and *Book 2*, Chapter 8 Number sequences.

Answers and Guidance

Question 11

Answer	How to work out the answer

a) 7   *1 mark*

STEP 1 Identify that what you need to know is the answer to this sum:

$\square \times 5 = 35$

STEP 2 Use your knowledge of your 5 times table to work out that the answer is:

$7 \times 5 = 35$

Answer	How to work out the answer

b) 24   *1 mark*

STEP 1 Identify that what you need to know is the answer to this sum:

$\square \div 6 = 4$

STEP 2 Recognise that to find the missing number you need to solve the sum:

$\square = 4 \times 6$

STEP 3 Use your knowledge of the 6 times table to work out the answer:

$24 = 4 \times 6$

Inside the Maths

You needed to:

- identify the mathematics you needed to solve problems
- know your tables very thoroughly
- be able to use your knowledge of tables in simple problems
- understand the relationship between division and multiplication.

See Collins Success in Maths Book 1, Chapter 5 Using multiplication and Chapter 10 Solving problems, and Book 3, Chapter 7 Missing numbers.

Question 12

Answer

$$3\overline{)78} \quad 26$$

1 mark

How to work out the answer

STEP 1 Work back from the end of the answer. In order for this to be 6, the 3 must have been divided into 18 since $18 \div 3 = 6$.

STEP 2 You now know that the remainder from dividing 3 into the missing number must be 1 to make the 8 into 18.

STEP 3 The missing number must be 7 since $7 \div 3 = 2$ remainder 1.

Or Use a 'trial and improvement' method.

STEP 1 Your first thought might be that 6 would be a good answer because $6 \div 3 = 2$.

STEP 2 Try it and see.

$$\begin{array}{r} 22 \quad r\,2 \\ 3\overline{)68} \end{array}$$

STEP 3 This answer is not big enough so try a larger number.

$$\begin{array}{r} 26 \\ 3\overline{)78} \\ \underline{6} \\ 18 \\ \underline{18} \\ 0 \end{array}$$

Inside the Maths

You needed to:

- understand division and know the correct way to write down a long division sum
- know the relationship between multiplication and division
- know how to use trial and improvement methods.

See Collins Success in Maths Book 2, Chapter 2 Division, Book 3, Chapter 7 Missing numbers and Book 4, Chapter 4 Solving problems and Chapter 5 Division.

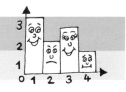

Question 13

Answer

£15   *2 marks*

How to work out the answer

 Identify how much each child raised.

Louise	£3
Hassan	£5
David	£4
Sarah	£7
Donna	£6

 Add these amounts together to find the total amount raised = £25.

 Subtract this amount from £40 to find out how much more needs to be raised.

£40 – £25 = £15

Remember to write down all your working as you go along. You might get 1 mark even if you made a mistake in the calculation.

Inside the Maths

You needed to be able to:

 read a bar graph

 identify the mathematics you needed

use addition and subtraction in solving problems.

See Collins Success in Maths Book 1, Chapter 4 Missing numbers, Chapter 9 Using bar graphs and Chapter 10 Solving problems

Question 14

Answer

a) 100 cm   *1 mark*

How to work out the answer

 Count the number of 5 cm sides that make up the outer edge of the ring. There are 20.

 20 × 5 cm = 100 cm

Answer

b) 6 squares   *1 mark*

How to work out the answer

 Visualise the complete ring. If you find this difficult, you could sketch in the missing part.

You can see that you have 2 extra squares.

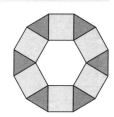

 Count **all** the squares!

Inside the Maths

You needed to:

 know what a perimeter is and how to calculate it

 read the question and answer the question you were asked. Many marks are lost in the National Test through failing to read the question properly.

See Collins Success in Maths Book 1, Chapter 8 Perimeters and Book 3 Chapter 8 Area and perimeter.

Answers and Guidance

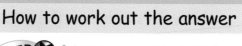

Question 15

Answer

100 55 10 **–35** **–80**   *2 marks*
            (1 for each correct number)

How to work out the answer

 **STEP 1** Subtract or count back 45 from 10. Take care when you get to zero. If you find this difficult, you could draw yourself a number line to help.

```
←|..|..|..|..|..|..|..|..|..|..|..|..|..|..|..|..|..|..|..|→
 −80 −70 −60 −50 −40 −30 −20 −10  0  10  20  30  40  50  60  70  80  90  100
```

Inside the Maths

You needed to be able to work with numbers less than zero (negative numbers), either mentally or by using a number line.

See *Collins Success in Maths Book 3*, Chapter 5 Negative numbers.

Question 16

Answer

a) Approximately $\frac{1}{4}$

You were asked for a fraction so you could also have written the decimal fraction 0.25 but you could not answer 25%.

Answers between $\frac{1}{5}$ (0.2) and $\frac{3}{10}$ (0.3) would also be allowed.

1 mark

How to work out the answer

Either:

 STEP 1 Take a good look at the different sizes of the bands and estimate what fraction of the total height is taken up by the 'organic' band.

Or:

 STEP 1 Measure the total height (in cm) and the height of the 'organic' band, and calculate the fraction. You need to round the numbers otherwise the calculation is very difficult.

Answer

b) 17.5 kg

Answers between 16 kg and 19 kg are also acceptable.

1 mark

How to work out the answer

 STEP 1 Estimate how much smaller the 'glass and metal' band is than the 'plastic' band, either by sight or by measurement.
It is roughly half so they throw away approximately half of 35 kilograms.

 STEP 2 $\frac{1}{2}$ of 35 = 17.5

Answer

c) 91 kg

2 marks

How to work out the answer

 STEP 1 Recognise that 130 kg is 100% of the paper and card that is thrown away.

 STEP 2 Calculate 1% of 130 kg. $\frac{130}{100} = 1.3$

 STEP 3 Calculate 70% of 130 kg. 1.3×70
$= 1.3 \times 10 \times 7 = 13 \times 7 = 91$ kg

Inside the Maths

You needed to be able to:

 estimate fractions of shapes

 calculate a fraction of a quantity

 calculate percentages.

The work is also similar to that on circular pie charts.

See *Collins Success in Maths Book 3*, Chapter 11 Percentages and Chapter 12 Pie charts, and *Book 4*, Chapter 1 Fractions of shapes.

Question 17

Answer

a) $\frac{1}{8}$ *1 mark*

How to work out the answer

 STEP 1 Count the number of divisions or segments on spinner A. There are 8.

Count the number of 4s on spinner A. There is 1.

STEP 2 The probability of spinning a 4 is therefore 1 out of 8 which you should write as $\frac{1}{8}$.

Note that you were asked for a fraction so 1 : 8 or 1 in 8 or 1 out of 8 would not be correct. You could, however, have given the decimal fraction which is 0.125.

Answer

b) B

To get the mark you would also need to have an explanation like one of these.

- 'Because there is a $\frac{3}{8}$ chance of spinning a 1 on spinner A and a $\frac{2}{4}$ ($\frac{1}{2}$) chance of spinning a 1 on spinner B. $\frac{2}{4}$ is bigger than $\frac{3}{8}$.'

- 'Because there is more space on spinner B than on spinner A where the arrow might land on a 1.'

The first explanation is more mathematical and is the better answer but both are correct. Get an adult to check that your answer is clear. The answer must include a **comparison between the two spinners**. An answer such as 'Because there is a big space on spinner B' would not get any marks.   *1 mark*

c) Your answer should be like one of these.

- 'The chance of spinning a 2 on spinner A is $\frac{2}{8} = \frac{1}{4}$. On spinner B it is $\frac{1}{4}$ so there is the same (equal) chance of spinning a 2.'

- 'The spinners are the same size and there is the same amount of space for 2 on both spinners.'   *1 mark*

How to work out the answer

 STEP 1 Count the number of divisions on spinner A. There are 8.
Count the number of 1s on spinner A. There are 3.

 STEP 2 The probability of spinning a 1 on spinner A is $\frac{3}{8}$.

 STEP 3 Count the number of divisions on spinner B. There are 4.
Count the number of 1s on spinner B. There are 2.

 STEP 4 The probability of spinning a 1 on spinner B is $\frac{2}{4}$ or $\frac{1}{2}$.

 STEP 5 Compare the probabilities. $\frac{2}{4}$ is bigger than $\frac{3}{8}$ so you are more likely to spin a 1 on spinner B.

The steps for working out part (c) are the same as for part (b). Ask an adult to check that your explanation is clear.

Inside the Maths

You needed to be able to:

- calculate probabilities and express them as fractions
- compare probabilities
- write a clear explanation of your mathematical thinking.

See Collins Success in Maths Book 3, Chapter 2 Probability and Chapter 6 Fractions

Answers and Guidance

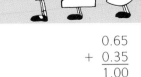

Question 18

Answer

0.1 (0.65) 0.99 0.45 (0.35)   *1 mark*

Inside the Maths

You need to be able to:

 add numbers, including decimals

work very systematically

understand the importance of
checking your answers.

See *Collins Success in Maths Book 2,*
Chapter 4 Adding and subtracting
decimals.

How to work out the answer

STEP 1 Look along the line and see if you can
recognise the answer easily.
If you can, check by adding.

```
  0.65
+ 0.35
  1.00
     1
```

STEP 2 If you do not recognise the answer, work systematically. Start at the
first number (0.1) and check it with each of the other numbers in turn.

It is obviously not 0.1 + 0.65 or 0.1 + 0.45 or
0.1 + 0.35 but it just could be 0.1 + 0.99. If you
are not sure, check by doing an addition sum.

```
   0.1
+ 0.99
  1.09
     1
```

So 0.1 is not in the answer.

STEP 3 Look at the next number (0.65). Check it with the other numbers.
It is obviously not 0.65 + 0.1 (you have checked this already) or
0.65 + 0.99 but it might be 0.65 + 0.45 or 0.65 + 0.35.

STEP 4 Check these two possibilities
by doing these addition sums.

```
  0.65        0.65
+ 0.45      + 0.35
  1.10        1.00
```

Question 19

Answer

15 trays   *2 marks*

Inside the Maths

 You needed to understand
division.

See *Collins Success in Maths Book 2,*
Chapter 2 Division and *Book 4,*
Chapter 5 Division.

How to work out the answer

STEP 1 Recognise that if there are 12 eggs per tray and 180 eggs
altogether, then there are 180 ÷ 12 trays.

STEP 2 Carry out the division sum:

```
        15
  12)180
      12
      60
      60
       0
```

Question 20

Answer

14 204   *2 marks*

Inside the Maths

 You needed to be able to do
long multiplication.

See *Collins Success in Maths Book 3,*
Chapter 3 Multiplying larger numbers.

How to work out the answer

STEP 1 There are several different ways of
doing this multiplication without
a calculator. Here is one example.
Use the method that you are
most comfortable with – probably
the one you were taught in school.

```
    268
  ×  53
  13 400    (50 × 268)
     804    (3 × 268)
  14 204    (13 400 + 804)
```

Your overall marks for Test A [   ]   Total possible marks for Test A [37]

You MAY use a calculator to answer any questions in this test.

1 On sports day children get points for how far they jump.

Standing Long Jump		
Over	80 cm	1 point
Over	100 cm	2 points
Over	120 cm	3 points
Over	140 cm	4 points
Over	160 cm	5 points
Over	180 cm	6 points

Joe jumped 138 cm.

How many points does he get?

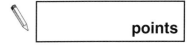

points

1 mark

Sam said, '*I jumped 1.5 metres. I get 4 points*.'

Give a reason why Sam is correct.

....

....

....

1 mark

Each child puts a cross on a line to show how far they jumped.

Sam puts her cross at 1.5 metres.

Lynn jumps **1.14** metres.

Put a cross on the line for Lynn's jump.

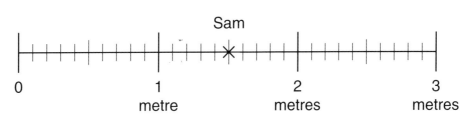

1 mark

25

2 There are 39 cheese sandwiches.

A cheese sandwich costs 45p.

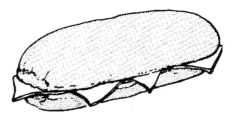

Use your calculator to work out the cost of 39 cheese sandwiches.

What is the number in your calculator display? Write it here.

1 mark

Write your answer in pounds.

£

1 mark

3 Here are five shapes on a square grid.

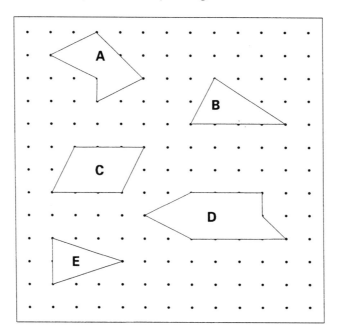

Write in the **missing** letters.

Shape ☐ has two pairs of parallel sides.

1 mark

Shape ☐ is a pentagon.

1 mark

Shape ☐ has reflective symmetry.

1 mark

4 Here is an **equilateral triangle** drawn on a circle.

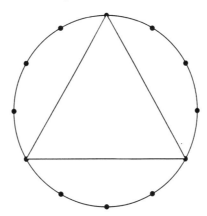

Use a ruler to draw a **regular hexagon** on this circle.

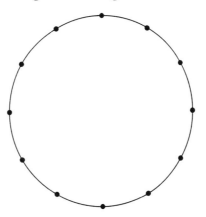

1 mark

5 Here is a map of an island.

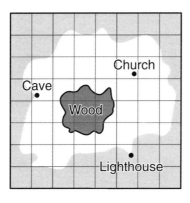

Estimate the area of the **Wood**.

squares

1 mark

6   Millie and Ryan play a number game.

What's my number?

Is it under 20?	Yes
Is it a multiple of 3?	Yes
Is it a multiple of 5?	Yes

What is the number?

1 mark

They play the game again.

Is it under 20?	No
Is it under 25?	Yes
Is it odd?	Yes
Is it a prime number?	Yes

What is the number?

1 mark

7   Calculate $\frac{7}{8}$ of **5000**

1 mark

8 Amy and Tom are given this number puzzle.

> **Find the two numbers which add up to 10 and make 20 when multiplied together.**

Amy guesses **7.3** and **2.7**

$$7.3 + 2.7 = 10$$
and $7.3 \times 2.7 = 19.71$ (too small)

Tom guesses **7.1** and **2.9**

$$7.1 + 2.9 = 10$$
and $7.1 \times 2.9 = 20.59$ (too big)

Make a **better** guess than Amy and Tom.

 and

1 mark

Use a calculator to check your guess.

☐ + ☐ = ☐

☐ × ☐ = ☐

1 mark

Make an **even better** guess than the last one.

☐ and ☐

1 mark

9 This three-digit number has **2** and **7** as **factors**.

2 9 4

Write another **three-digit** number which has **2** and **7** as **factors**.

1 mark

10 These shapes have been sorted.

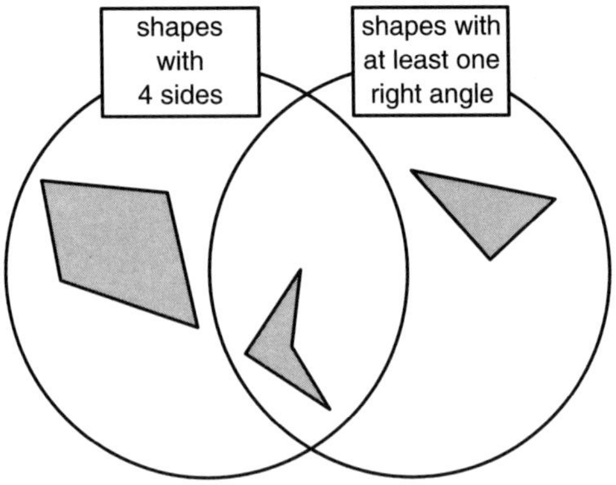

shapes with 4 sides

shapes with at least one right angle

Where does this shape belong?

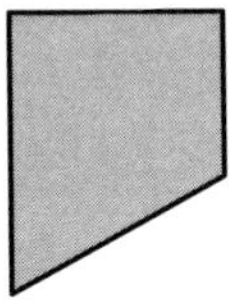

Draw it in its correct place.

1 mark

How did you decide? Give **TWO** reasons.

1. ....

....

1 mark

2. ....

....

1 mark

11 Here are the ingredients for fish pie for **two people**.

Omar makes fish pie for **3 people**.

How many **grams of fish** should he use?

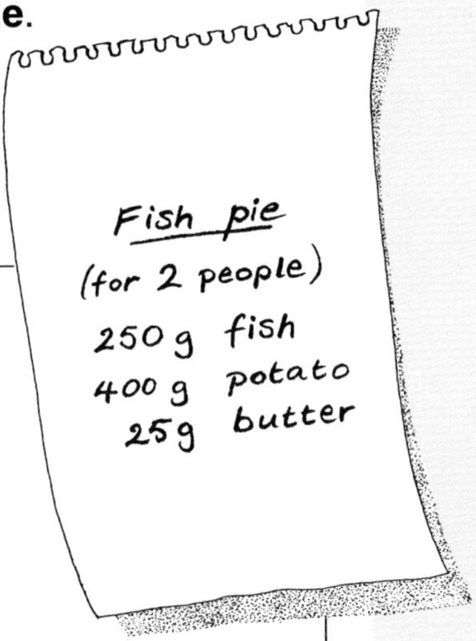

Show your **working**. You may get a mark.

Fish pie
(for 2 people)
250 g fish
400 g potato
25 g butter

g

2 marks

12 Here is a graph.

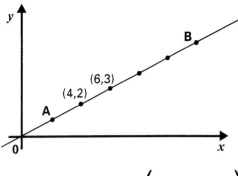

The dots (●) on the line are **equally spaced**.

What are the **co-ordinates** of the point **A**?   (,   )

1 mark

Megan says,

    'The point B has co-ordinates (11, 5).'

Use the graph to explain why she **cannot** be correct.

....

....

1 mark

13 Here is a drawing of a model car.

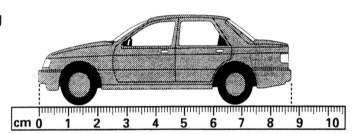

What is the **length** of the model?

Give your answer in **centimetres**, correct to one decimal place.

  [**cm**]

1 mark

The height of the model is **2.8 centimetres**.

The height of the real car is **50** times the height of the model.

What is the **height** of the **real car**? Give your answer in **metres**.

Show your **method**. You may get a mark.

[**m**]

2 marks

14 Here is a shaded shape on a grid made of squares.

Draw the **line of symmetry** of the **shaded shape**.

You may use a mirror or tracing paper.

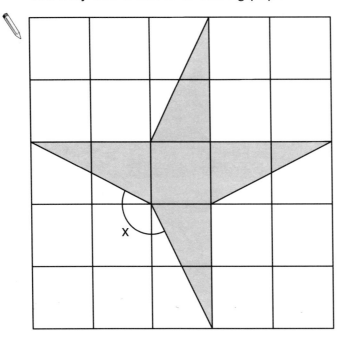

1 mark

What **fraction** of the area of the grid is shaded?

1 mark

Measure **angle x** in degrees.

Use an angle measurer (protractor).

1 mark

15 Here are two bags.

Each bag has **3 white balls** and **one black ball** in it.

A ball is taken from **one of the bags** without looking.

What is the probability that it is a **black ball**?

Give your answer as a fraction.

1 mark

All the balls from **both bags** are now mixed together in a new bag.

Put a cross (**✗**) on this line to show the probability of taking a black ball from the new bag.

```
|------|------|------|------|
0                           1
```

1 mark

16   Tom, Amy and Helen want to go on a boat trip.

There are three boats.

Lark	**Heron**	**Kestrel**
50 minute trip	70 minute trip	90 minute trip
Tickets £2.75 each	**Tickets £3.50 each**	**Tickets £4.20 each**

How much does it cost altogether for **three** people to go on the **Lark**?

£

1 mark

Tom and Amy go on the **Heron**.
They leave at **2.15pm**.

At what **time** do they return?

pm

1 mark

Helen goes on the **Kestrel** and **gets back at 4.15pm**.

At what **time** did the boat leave?

pm

1 mark

17 A shop sells sheets of sticky labels.

On each sheet there are **36 rows** and **18 columns** of labels.

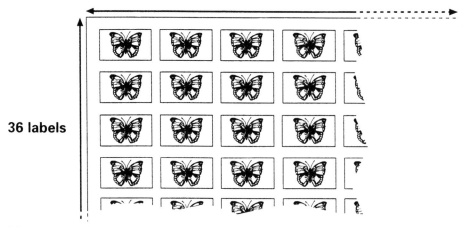

18 labels

36 labels

How many labels are there altogether on **45 sheets**?

Show your **method**. You may get a mark.

2 marks

18 The shaded shape is an **isosceles** triangle.

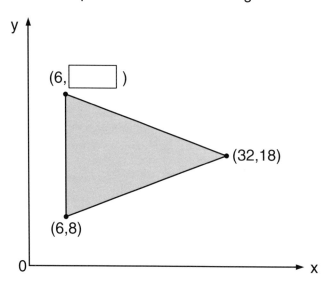

Write in the **missing co-ordinate**.

1 mark

19 Mr Jones has two sizes of square paving stones.

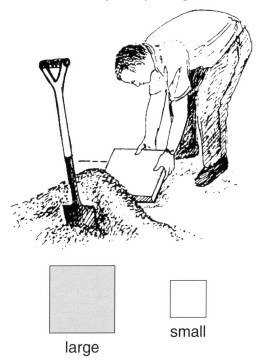

large   small

He uses them to make a path.

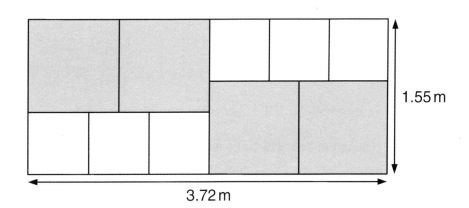

1.55 m

3.72 m

The path measures **1.55 metres** by **3.72 metres**.

Calculate the **width** of a **small paving stone**.

Show your **method**. You may get a mark.

2 marks

20 Strips of paper are each **30 centimetres** long.

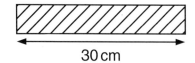

30 cm

Steve joins strips of paper together to make a **streamer**.

The strips overlap each other by **5 cm**.

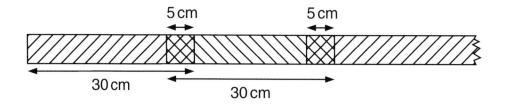

5 cm   5 cm

30 cm   30 cm

How long is a streamer made from
only 2 strips?

cm

1 mark

Sunita makes a streamer that is **280 cm** long.

How many **strips** does she use?

Show
your **working**.
You may get
a mark.

2 marks

36

Test B

Question 1

Answer

a) 3 points *1 mark*

b) Your answer should say or clearly imply that 1.5 metres is 150 cm and this is more than 140 cm but less than 160 cm so Sam scores 4 points. Ask an adult to check for you. *1 mark*

How to work out the answer

 Identify the column which gives the length of the jump.

 Identify that a jump of 138 cm is more than 120 cm and less than 140 cm.

 Look back to the points for jumping 120 cm (3 points). Joe jumped more than 120 cm but less than 140 cm so he gets 3 points. Use a similar method to work out part (b).

Answer

c)

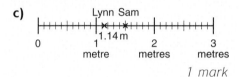

Lynn Sam
1.14 m
0   1   2   3
metre metres metres

1 mark

How to work out the answer

 Work out that each small division on the scale is 0.1 m.

 Identify that 1.14 m lies about halfway between 1.1 m and 1.2 m.

 Count 1 small division after the 1 m mark.

 Find the place that is almost halfway between this point on the scale and the next one. Put your cross here. Be sure to use a sharp pencil and mark the place very accurately.

Inside the Maths

You needed to know how to:

 read a table

 read scales accurately
convert units.

See Collins Success in Maths Book 1, Chapter 6 Number lines and scales and Book 3, Chapter 9 Conversion of units.

Question 2

Answer

1755 *1 mark*
£17.55 *1 mark*

How to work out the answer

 Key in   Display shows 1755
Check your answer by mentally rounding the numbers and making a rough estimate: $40 \times 50 = 2000$ or $40 \times 45 = 1800$

You would get a mark for writing £17.55p but this answer is not good mathematically. £17:55 and £17–55 would also be accepted.

Inside the Maths

You needed to be able to:

 use a calculator correctly
check calculator answers by making a sound estimate

 change an answer in pence to one expressed in pounds.

See Collins Success in Maths Book 1, Chapter 12 Using a calculator, Book 3, Chapter 9 Conversion of units and Book 4, Chapter 2 Using your calculator.

Answers and Guidance

Question 3

Answer

a) Shape C has two pairs of parallel sides. *1 mark*

How to work out the answer

 Remember that parallel sides are sides which are the same distance apart through their whole length (like railway lines).

Answer

b) Shape A is a pentagon. *1 mark*

How to work out the answer

 Remember that a pentagon has five sides.

Answer

c) Shape E has reflective symmetry. *1 mark*

How to work out the answer

 Remember that a shape has reflective symmetry when you can draw one or more mirror lines to split it into two exactly similar halves.

Inside the Maths

 You needed to know the meaning of a variety of vocabulary about shapes. In this question, you needed to know what the words 'parallel sides', 'pentagon' and 'reflective symmetry' meant.

See Collins Success in Maths Book 1, Chapter 11 Reflective symmetry and Book 2, Chapters 1 and 10 on shape.

Question 4

Answer

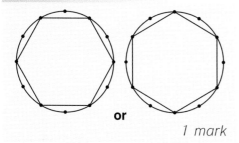

or

1 mark

How to work out the answer

 Identify that a hexagon has six sides. Note that the question asks for a **regular** hexagon, which means that all the sides must be the same length.

 If you cannot immediately see how to draw a hexagon, count the spaces between the dots round the edge of the circle. There are 12.

 Work out that each side must take up two spaces: 12 ÷ 6 = 2.

 Use a ruler to draw straight lines between alternate dots on the circle. Always draw maths diagrams with a sharp pencil.

Inside the Maths

You needed to be able to:

 draw accurate representations of shapes.

See Collins Success in Maths Book 1, Chapter 3 Drawing 2D shapes.

Question 5

Answer

4 squares *1 mark*

How to work out the answer

 Identify the area covered by the wood (dotted).

 Count the squares that are more than half covered (marked with ticks). There are four. Do not count the squares that are less than half covered.

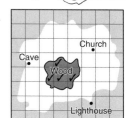

Inside the Maths

 You needed to be able to calculate area by counting squares.

See Collins Success in Maths Book 3, Chapter 8 Area and perimeter.

Question 6

Answer

a) 15   *1 mark*

How to work out the answer

 Identify the numbers under 20:

I, 2, 3, 4, 5, 6, 7, 8, 9, 10, 11, 12, 13, 14, 15, 16, 17, 18, 19

(You only need to write them down if you find it a help.)

 Identify which numbers are under 20 **and** in the 3 times table (multiples of 3):

3, 6, 9, 12, 15, 18

 Identify which of these numbers is also in the 5 times table (multiples of 5):

15 is the only one.

Answer

b) 23   *1 mark*

How to work out the answer

 Identify the numbers that are over 20 **and** under 25:

21, 22, 23, 24

 Identify which of these are odd numbers:

21 and 23

 Remember that a prime number is one that can only be divided by 1 and itself – it does not appear in any times table.
21 is in the 7 and 3 times table therefore it is **not** a prime number.
The only factors of 23 are 1 and 23 therefore it is a prime number.

Inside the Maths

You needed to:

 know a range of maths language – in this question you needed to understand 'multiple', 'odd' and 'prime number'

 work carefully and systematically through a set of instructions (or definitions).

See Collins Success in Maths Book 1, Chapter 10 Solving problems.

Question 7

Answer

4375   *1 mark*

How to work out the answer

 Calculate $\frac{1}{8}$ of 5000 by dividing 5000 by 8.

Find $\frac{7}{8}$ by multiplying your answer by 7.

It is much easier if you use a calculator.

Key in [AC] [5] [0] [0] [0] [÷] [8] [×] [7] [=]

Display shows 4375

If you did not use a calculator then your calculation may look like this.

```
      625                 625
  8)5000            ×       7
    48                   4375
    20
    16
    40
    40
    00
```

Inside the Maths

You needed to be able to:

 find a fraction of a whole number

 use a calculator correctly, including making estimates of answers.

See Collins Success in Maths Book 1, Chapter 12 Using a calculator and Book 3, Chapter 6 Fractions.

Answers and Guidance

Question 8

Answer

a) To be correct, your guess should use numbers between 7.1 and 7.3 and between 2.7 and 2.9. The most obvious answer is 7.2 and 2.8. *1 mark*

If you have a different answer ask an adult to check it for you.

How to work out the answer

STEP 1 Notice that Amy's guesses when multiplied together were too small, and that Tom's guesses when multiplied together were too big.

STEP 2 Realise that to obtain an answer to the multiplication sum that will be between Amy's and Tom's answers, you need to pick numbers between Amy's and Tom's numbers.

Answer

b) If you chose the same numbers that we did (7.2 and 2.8) then your answers would be:

7.2 + 2.8 = 10.00
and 7.2 × 2.8 = 20.16 *1 mark*

If you had different numbers you'll need to ask an adult to check for you.

How to work out the answer

STEP 1 Key in

Display shows 10.00

STEP 2 Key in

Display shows 20.16

Answer

c) To be correct, your answer needs to be an even better guess, your first number needs to be **between** 7.2 and 7.3 and your second number needs to be **between** 2.7 and 2.8. For example, you might chose 7.25 and 2.75.

1 mark

Remember your two numbers must still add up to 10.

You need to ask an adult to check for you if your guess is not the same as ours.

How to work out the answer

STEP 1 Identify whether the result of your guess in part (b) (the answer you obtained when you multiplied the two numbers together) was too large or too small.

STEP 2 Look at Amy's and Tom's original guesses. Notice that to get a bigger answer Tom used a smaller first number and a bigger second number than Amy did.

STEP 3 If your answer was too small, and you need to make it bigger, choose a first number that is **smaller** than the one you used in part (b), and a second number that is **larger** than the one that you used in part (b).

STEP 4 If it was too large, and you need to make it smaller, choose a first number that is **larger** than the one you used in part (b), and a second number that is **smaller** than the one that you used in part (b).

STEP 5 Check that the numbers you have chosen still add up to 10.

STEP 6 Realise that it doesn't matter if they do not make exactly 20 when multiplied together – we are still making 'better guesses'.

Inside the Maths

You needed to be able to:

 to use a calculator

 use 'trial and improvement' methods to solve problems.

See Collins Success in Maths Book 4, Chapter 2 Using your calculator and Chapter 4 Solving problems.

Question 9

Answer

There are lots of possible answers to this question. Ask an adult to check your answer for you. Remember, you must be able to divide it by 2 so it must be an even number and it must also be divisible by 7. *1 mark*

Inside the Maths

You needed to be able to:

 use 'trial and improvement' methods

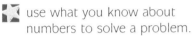 use what you know about numbers to solve a problem.

See Collins Success in Maths Book 4, Chapter 4 Solving problems.

How to work out the answer

Either use a trial and improvement method for this question.

 STEP 1 Recognise that you need to find an even three-digit number divisible by 7. Choose any three-digit even number (except 294) for example:

$$264 \div 7 \qquad 7\overline{)264} \quad \begin{array}{c}37\\ \end{array} \text{ r 5}$$

 STEP 2 Add 2 on to 264 (you had a remainder of 5 so adding 2 would make another complete 7):

$$266 \div 7 \qquad 7\overline{)266} \quad 38 \qquad 266 \text{ is one correct solution.}$$

Or

 STEP 1 Realise that you know 294 is divisible by 7 so add another 7.

 STEP 2 Recognise that 301 is also divisible by 7 but it is not even and is not therefore divisible by 2.

 STEP 3 Add another 7. 308 is divisible by 7 and is also even and divisible by 2, so 308 is another correct solution.

Question 10

Answer

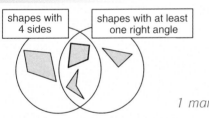

1 mark

Ask an adult to check your answers. Here are two examples.
1. The shape has 4 sides so it goes in 'shapes with 4 sides'. *1 mark*
2. The shape has two right angles so it also goes in 'shapes with at least one right angle'. *1 mark*

How to work out the answer

 STEP 1 Follow the two reasons given opposite.

 STEP 2 Identify that to be in both sets (circles) the shape must be in the overlap of the sets. This is called the 'intersection' of the sets.

Inside the Maths

You needed to know:

 the vocabulary used to describe shape – in this case, 'right angle'

 how to show data in a Venn diagram.

See Collins Success in Maths Book 2, Chapter 1 Properties of shape.

Question 11

Answer

375 g *2 marks*

Inside the Maths

You needed to be able to:

 Think clearly to decide what steps you needed to take to solve the problem.

How to work out the answer

 STEP 1 Notice that the ingredients are for 2 people.

 STEP 2 Work out how much fish you need for 1 person by dividing the quantity in the recipe by 2:

$$250 \div 2 = 125 g \text{ or } \frac{250}{2} = 125 g$$

 **STEP 3** Now work out how much you need for 3 people:

$$3 \times 125 g = 375 g$$

Answers and Guidance

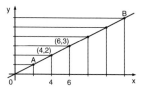

Answer

How to work out the answer

a) (2, 1)   *1 mark*

 Visualise – or draw – lines on the graph.

 In each pair of numbers, identify the co-ordinate which refers to the horizontal axis (the x-axis). This is the first number in each pair. Visualise or write the x-co-ordinates on the horizontal axis.

 Identify the y-co-ordinates (the second number in each pair). Visualise or write these on the vertical axis (the y-axis).

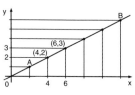

 Since you have been told that the dots are equally spaced you can identify the size of the 'gaps' between the co-ordinates on each axis.

On the x-axis, the gap between the points you know (4 and 6) is 2 so the other points are 2, 8, 10, 12.

On the y-axis, the gap between the points you know (2 and 3) is 1 so the other points are 1, 4, 5, 6.

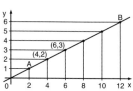

 You can now see that the co-ordinates for A are (2, 1).

Answer

How to work out the answer

b) Megan **cannot** be correct because (here are some examples of acceptable answers):
- the x-co-ordinate is always even and 11 is an odd number
- the actual co-ordinates of point B are (12, 6)
- the y-co-ordinate is always half the x-co-ordinate and 5 is not half of 11.   *1 mark*

 Your reason needed to show that you:
- know that the x-co-ordinate is always even **or**
- know that the co-ordinates of point B are (12, 6) **or**
- recognise that the second co-ordinate is always half of the first one.

Inside the Maths

You needed to be able to read, write and use co-ordinates in problems.

See *Collins Success in Maths Book 2*, Chapter 7 Co-ordinates.

Answer

How to work out the answer

a) 8.7 cm   *1 mark*

 Identify that, as the scale is marked in whole centimetres, each sub-division is 'worth' a tenth (0.1) of a centimetre.

 Read the scale, counting the sub-divisions carefully. Remember that the instruction is to give the answer to one decimal place (1dp). This means there should be one figure after the decimal point.

Answer

b) 1.4 metres   *2 marks*

Inside the Maths

You needed to be able to:

 read a scale

 convert metric units.

See Collins Success in Maths Book 1, Chapter 6 Number lines and scales and Book 3, Chapter 9 Conversion of units.

How to work out the answer

 Multiply the height of the model (2.8 cm) by 50. The height of the car is 140 cm.

 Convert 140 cm into metres. There are 100 centimetres in a metre so divide 140 by 100. The car is 1.4 metres high.

You might have noticed that you could do these calculations directly:

$$2.8 \, cm \times \frac{50}{100} = 1.4 \text{ metres}$$

 You should check that your answer is sensible by thinking about the height of a real car and making an estimate. This should help prevent you from giving answers such as 14 metres (about the height of two double-decker buses!) or 0.14 metres (about the length of a pencil!)

Question 14

Answer

a)

1 mark

How to work out the answer

 Remember that the mirror line divides the shape into two identical halves, each the exact reflection of the other.

Answer

b) $\frac{1}{5}$ *1 mark*

How to work out the answer

 Count the squares that are more than half shaded – do not count those that are less than half shaded.

Or

Notice that some parts of the shape go together to make whole squares. The equivalent of five squares are shaded.

 Count the total number of squares in the grid. There are 25.

 Calculate the fraction of squares that are shaded: $\frac{5}{25}$.

 Reduce the fraction to its simplest form by dividing the top and bottom numbers by 5. $\frac{5}{25} = \frac{1}{5}$

Answer

c) The angle is 150°.   *1 mark*

How to work out the answer

 Put your protractor over the diagram with the centre point as shown. Make sure you line it up accurately. Check which scale you are using by making sure you work up from the 0 (zero) point.

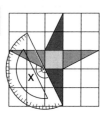

Inside the Maths

You needed to know about:

 reflective symmetry

 calculating area by counting squares

 calculating area by shape

 measuring angles.

See Collins Success in Maths Book 1, Chapter 3 Drawing 2D shapes and Chapter 11 Reflective symmetry and Book 3, Chapter 8 Area and perimeter.

Answers and Guidance

Question 15

Answer

a) $\frac{1}{4}$ *1 mark*

How to work out the answer

STEP 1 There are four balls in each bag, only one is black so there is a one in four chance of drawing a black ball.

STEP 2 'One in four' expressed as a fraction is $\frac{1}{4}$.

Remember you **must** use a fraction to express your answer as you were instructed. You will not get a mark for '1 out of 4' or '1 in 4' or '1 : 4'. You **would** get a mark for writing it as a decimal fraction (0.25).

Answer

b)

               1 mark

How to work out the answer

STEP 1 There are 8 balls in the bag. Since two are black you have two chances out of eight of drawing a black ball.

STEP 2 Two out of eight, written as a fraction is $\frac{2}{8}$.

STEP 3 $\frac{2}{8} = \frac{1}{4}$.

STEP 4 Mark the point $\frac{1}{4}$ of the way between 0 (no chance) and 1 (certainty).

Inside the Maths

You needed to be able to:

- understand simple probabilities
- write probabilities as fractions
- reduce a fraction to its simplest form.

You also needed to read the question carefully and answer it exactly as you were told to do remembering to express the probabilities as fractions.

See *Collins Success in Maths Book 1*, Chapter 7 Probability, Book 2, Chapter 11 Equivalent fractions and *Book 3*, Chapter 2 Probability

Question 16

Answer

a) £8.25   *1 mark*

How to work out the answer

STEP 1 Identify that it costs £2.75 for each person.

STEP 2 Multiply £2.75 by 3. It is much better to do this with a calculator.

STEP 3 Make a rough estimate to check your calculator answer. £3 × 3 = £9 is about the right size. Doing this stops you making a mistake with where you put the decimal point.

Answer

b) 3.25 pm   *1 mark*

How to work out the answer

STEP 1 Identify that it takes 70 minutes to take a trip on Heron.

STEP 2 70 minutes = 1 hour and 10 minutes

STEP 3 Add 1 hour 10 minutes to 2.15 pm to reach 3.25 pm.

Answer

c) 2.45 pm   *1 mark*

How to work out the answer

 Identify that it takes 90 minutes to take a trip on Kestrel. 90 minutes = 1 hour and 30 minutes

 Subtract 1 hour and 30 minutes from 4.15 pm.
4.15 pm – 1 hour 30 minutes = 3.15 pm – 30 minutes = 2.45 pm

Inside the Maths

You needed to be able to:

 solve problems involving money including multiplication of money

solve problems involving time

use a calculator correctly and make estimates of answers.

See Collins Success in Maths Book 1, Chapter 2 Using timetables, Chapter 5 Using multiplication and Chapter 12 Using a calculator, and Book 4, Chapter 9 Time.

Question 17

Answer

29 160   *2 marks*

Inside the Maths

You needed to know:

how to use a calculator

how to do long multiplication.

See Collins Success in Maths Book 4, Chapter 2 Using your calculator.

How to work out the answer

 Recognise that there are 18 × 36 labels on one sheet.
So there are 18 × 36 × 45 labels on 45 sheets.
Make sure you write down how to do the sum so that you will still get a mark even if you make a mistake with the calculation.

 Using a calculator makes it easier and quicker.
Key in `AC` `1` `8` `×` `3` `6` `×` `4` `5` `=`
Display shows 29 160

 Check the size of your answer by making a rough estimate.

Question 18

Answer

(6, 28)   *1 mark*

Inside the Maths

You needed to know:

the properties of an isosceles triangle

how to use and write co-ordinates.

See Collins Success in Maths Book 2, Chapter 1 Properties of Shape and Chapter 7 Co-ordinates.

How to work out the answer

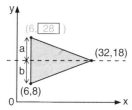

 Recall the properties of an isosceles triangle. There is a mirror line through the middle vertex.

 Note that the distance from the bottom vertex to the mirror line (marked b) is the same as the distance from the mirror line to the upper vertex (marked a). Also, the mirror line is parallel to the x-axis.

 The lower vertex is at (6, 8). The middle vertex is at (32, 18).

We are only interested in the y-co-ordinate (since this is the one that is missing). This is always the second number in a pair of co-ordinates.

 By subtracting the y-co-ordinate of the bottom vertex from the y-co-ordinate for the middle vertex we can calculate distance b.
18 – 8 = 10   This is the same as distance a.

 The y-co-ordinate for the top vertex is, therefore
8 + a + b = 8 + 10 + 10 = 28

 The full co-ordinates for the top vertex are (6, **28**).

Answers and Guidance

Answer

0.62 metres   *2 marks*

Inside the Maths

You needed to be able to:

 make good use of the information you are given

 divide decimal numbers.

See *Collins Success in Maths Book 2,*
Chapter 4 Adding and subtracting
decimals.

How to work out the answer

There are several ways of solving this problem. Here are two.

 Notice that the length of the path is 3.72 m.

See that three small stones make up the half the length of the path so the total length of three small stones = 3.72 ÷ 2 = 1.86 m.

 So the width of one small stone is 1.86 ÷ 3 = 0.62 m.

Or

 Notice that six small stones make up the total length of the path (3.72 m).

 See that the width of one small stone is 3.72 m ÷ 6 = 0.62 m.

Remember, whichever method you use, show your working. You may get a mark even if you make a mistake in the calculation.

Question 20

Answer

a) 55 cm   *1 mark*

How to work out the answer

 Make a sketch of the problem and mark in the lengths.

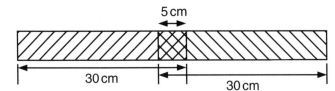

 You need to add the total length of 1 strip (30 cm) to the length of the second strip minus the length of the overlap (30 – 5). 30 + 25 = 55

Answer

b) Sunita uses 11 strips   *2 mark*

Inside the Maths

 You needed to be able to use the four rules of number together.

See *Collins Success in Maths Book 2,*
Chapter 6 Using symbols.

How to work out the answer

 Look for the rule. If you put another strip on to your sketch for part a of this question, you would add 30 cm **minus** the overlap. This is true for the fourth strip and any more that you add after that.
The rule is that you start with one 30 cm strip. Every other strip adds 25 cm to the total length.

 To find how many strips Sunita uses, subtract the length of the first 30 cm strip from the total length of the streamer.

280 – 30 = 250 cm

 Then find out how many 25 cm lengths make up the **rest** of the streamer.

250 ÷ 25 = 10 strips

 Remember to add in the first strip. Sunita used 11 strips.

Your overall marks for Test B [   ]   Total possible marks for Test B 43

46

Mental Arithmetic Test

Test questions

'For this first group of questions, you will have 5 seconds to work out each answer and write it down.'

	The questions	Answers	
1	How many twenty pence pieces are there in two pounds?	**10**	
2	Subtract forty from one hundred and twenty	**80**	
3	Multiply seven by nine.	**63**	
4	How would quarter past four in the afternoon be shown on a twenty-four hour digital clock?	**16:15**	Accept 16–15 or 1615 or 16 15 or sixteen fifteen. Do not accept 4.15 pm
5	How many millilitres are there in two and a half litres?	**2500** ml	

'For the next group of questions, you will have 10 seconds to work out each answer and write it down.'

6	Jan buys a newspaper for eighty pence and pays with a five pound note. How much change does she get?	**£4.20**	
7	What is twice five hundred and forty?	**1080**	
8	A bus is due to arrive at nine-fifty. It is twenty-five minutes late. At what time will it arrive?	**10:15**	Accept 10–15 or 10 15 or 1015 or quarter past 10, with or without am or pm.
9	A square playground has a perimeter of 100 metres. How long is one of its sides?	**25 m**	
10	Add three point five to four point eight.	**8.3**	
11	Imagine a triangular prism. How many faces does it have?	**5**	
12	The sequence of numbers on your answer sheet follows the rule double and subtract one. What is the next number?	**33**	
13	Put a ring around the fraction on your sheet which is equivalent to forty per cent.	$\frac{1}{40}$ $\frac{40}{40}$ $\frac{1}{4}$ $\boxed{\frac{4}{10}}$ $\frac{1}{400}$	
14	Calculate the difference between three hundred and forty and seven hundred and ten.	**370**	
15	When rolling a fair dice numbered one to six, what is the probability of getting an odd number?	$\frac{1}{2}$ or $\frac{3}{6}$	Accept also 50% or 0.5. Do not accept answers in words, eg '3 in 6' or '3 out of 6' or 'evens' or as a ratio, eg 1:2 or 3:6

'For the next group of questions, you will have 15 seconds to work out each answer and write it down.'

16	Add together thirty-eight, twenty-three and forty-four	**105**	
17	In a sale, there is fifty per cent off all prices. A chair costs forty-five pounds in the sale. How much was it before the sale?	**£90**	
18	What number is half-way between twenty-four and forty?	**32**	
19	The pie chart on your answer sheet shows the favourite colours of one hundred and twenty children. Use the chart to estimate the number of children who chose red.	**30** children	Accept answers in range 27 to 33 inclusive
20	Put a ring around the expression on the answer sheet which gives the answer nearest to 100.	50 × 19 49 × 20 $\boxed{1.9 \times 50}$ 4.9 × 19 5.9 × 20	

'Now put down your pen or pencil. The test is finished.'

Your overall marks for the mental test		Total possible marks for the mental test	20
Your overall marks for all tests		Total possible marks for all tests	100

Mental Arithmetic Test

Pupil answer sheet

Time: 5 seconds

1		20p

2		40 120

3	

4	

5		ml	$2\frac{1}{2}$ litres

Time: 10 seconds

6		80p

7		540

8		9:50 25

9		m

10		3.5 4.8

11	

Time: 10 seconds

12	3 5 9 17 ___

13	$\frac{1}{40}$ $\frac{40}{60}$ $\frac{1}{2}$ $\frac{4}{10}$ $\frac{1}{400}$

14		340 710

15	

Time: 15 seconds

16		38 23 44

17	£	£45

18		24 40

19	children

yellow
green
others
red
blue

120 children

20	50×19 49×20 1.9×50 4.9×1.9 5.9×20

Note to parents: Photocopy this sheet so that your child can write the answers on it while you read out the test.